MW01257745

Where Is Tornado Alley?

by Wes Locher

illustrated by Dede Putra

Penguin Workshop

To my own tornadoes, Amanda and Emmie—WL

PENGUIN WORKSHOP
An imprint of Penguin Random House LLC
1745 Broadway, New York, New York 10019

First published in the United States of America by Penguin Workshop,
an imprint of Penguin Random House LLC, 2025

Visit us online at penguinrandomhouse.com.

Library of Congress Cataloging-in-Publication Data is available.

Printed in the United States of America

ISBN 9780593752197 (paperback)   10 9 8 7 6 5 4 3 2 1 CJKW
ISBN 9780593752203 (library binding)   10 9 8 7 6 5 4 3 2 1 CJKW

Contents

Where Is Tornado Alley?

Captain Robert Miller was the meteorologist (an expert on weather forecasting) on duty the evening of March 20, 1948, at Tinker Air Force Base in central Oklahoma. While he had alerted the base of approaching wind gusts of thirty-five miles per hour, he didn't realize that the otherwise quiet evening he had predicted would soon be turned upside down when a tornado would rip through the base later that night.

The tornado (also sometimes called a "twister") raced through the Oklahoma City countryside before striking Tinker at 10:22 p.m. The funnel battered buildings and destroyed fifty-four aircraft. Airplanes left outside of hangars were tossed around like toys. Tools and airplane parts became dangerous objects in the fierce wind. After crashing through the base, the tornado disappeared. In the blink of an eye, the storm had caused more than $10 million in damage. The next morning, soldiers surveyed the destruction with amazement. How could the tornado have struck without warning? Nothing like it had ever happened before at Tinker. The US Air Force couldn't afford for it to happen again.

Robert Miller

The following day, Major Ernest Fawbush and Captain Robert Miller were tasked with examining past storms and weather patterns in the area. It was up to them to help find a way for Tinker Air Force Base not to be caught off guard by another tornado.

This wasn't an easy task. Fawbush and Miller didn't have access to the computer technology of today. In the 1940s, people relied on hand-drawn weather maps, crude weather-balloon information, and other charts and graphs for their research.

For the next several days, Fawbush and Miller studied past tornado-producing storms in Oklahoma. They hoped to reveal a pattern to the weather statistics they had on file that would let them predict tornadoes. If they could predict storms, the men could provide advance warning to the military bases around the country.

Perhaps Fawbush and Miller could even expand their work to help warn towns and cities. The pair felt a personal responsibility to prevent destruction and save lives.

Tinker Air Force Base sits directly in what Fawbush and Miller would later come to call "Tornado Alley." The term refers to a strip of land starting in Texas that stretches north through the states of Oklahoma, Kansas, Colorado, Nebraska, Iowa, and South Dakota.

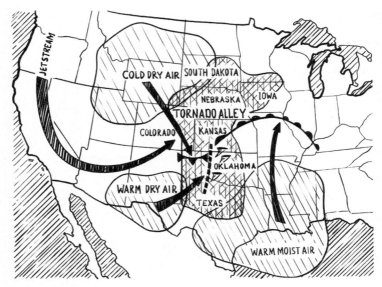

Tornado Alley

There are no official boundaries for Tornado Alley. The nickname simply refers to an approximately 500,000-square-mile area within the United States.

There are four elements at work in Tornado Alley that make it a perfect place for twisters to form. The upper atmosphere is home to a strong jet stream—the winds that form between pockets of warm and cold air. While cold, dry air blows down from Canada, warm, dry air travels north from Mexico. Those air masses soon meet the moist air drifting in from the Gulf of Mexico. Because Tornado Alley sits in a lowland region, there are few physical barriers—like mountains—to block or redirect the airflow. As these air masses collide over the entire area of Tornado Alley, they create the perfect recipe for sudden and dangerous storms.

After days of reviewing weather reports, Fawbush and Miller found the pattern they sought.

Minutes before each tornado had touched down in the state of Oklahoma, the weather patterns on the map appeared eerily similar. The two men felt confident they could predict a tornado, but they'd have to wait for another severe storm to put their theory to the test.

And they didn't have to wait long.

Five days later, on March 25, Fawbush and Miller paid close attention to the weather as another storm brewed nearby. The men recognized the telltale weather patterns that they associated with the birth of a tornado. They had to act.

Fawbush and Miller begged their commanding general, Fred Borum, to issue a tornado forecast for Tinker Air Force Base. Borum resisted. He knew that if he issued the warning and a tornado didn't touch down, soldiers wouldn't take future warnings seriously.

General Fred Borum

The meteorologists were faced with a difficult choice: They could keep quiet and risk even more tornado damage, or they could push the general to issue the tornado warning in hopes of saving lives.

Fawbush and Miller knew exactly what they had to do.

CHAPTER 1
The History of Meteorology

It seems that for as long as humans have been around, they have been intrigued by the weather and how to predict it. Throughout history, many great minds have studied the weather, a practice which came to be known as meteorology.

The first known meteorologist (someone who studies the weather) is thought to have been the Greek philosopher Aristotle.

Aristotle took an interest in big concepts including philosophy and the weather. In 340 BC, he wrote a book titled *Meteorologica*. It contains one of the earliest explanations of Earth's atmosphere (the layer of gases that surround planet Earth). However, that wasn't Aristotle's only major contribution.

His theories that the Earth was round, that the moon orbited the planet, and that Earth consisted of four main elements—earth, wind, fire, and air—were widely accepted by astronomers of his time.

Even before Aristotle, the ancient Egyptians believed they could control the weather and often held rituals to summon rain. (These were not always successful.)

Many ancient cultures who lived hundreds of years after Aristotle, and didn't have access to his writing, believed the weather was controlled by gods.

The Maya living in Central America looked to Chaac, their god of rain, thunder, and lightning.

Chaac

These early Mesoamerican people believed that Chaac carried a lightning ax, and when he struck the clouds, it created thunder and rain.

Between the years AD 300 and 900, the Maya developed their own systems of science, astronomy, architecture, timekeeping, and meteorology. They observed the skies and recorded what they saw over hundreds of years. As time went on, they recognized weather patterns and planetary movements. Soon, the Maya were predicting weather with greater accuracy.

As Aristotle's *Meteorologica* was translated to more and more languages, it was used as the basis of meteorology right up to and through the seventeenth century. There were still several inventions coming that would help take weather prediction from a dream to a reality.

The first of those important inventions was the barometer.

A barometer is a scientific instrument used by meteorologists to measure the rise and fall of atmospheric pressure, which is air pressure within the atmosphere.

A 1643 barometer

This tool helps predict the weather by indicating if a storm is going toward or away from a town or city.

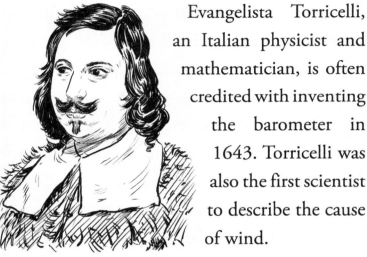

Evangelista Torricelli

Evangelista Torricelli, an Italian physicist and mathematician, is often credited with inventing the barometer in 1643. Torricelli was also the first scientist to describe the cause of wind.

The second invention to change meteorology forever was the thermometer, a tool for measuring variations in temperature.

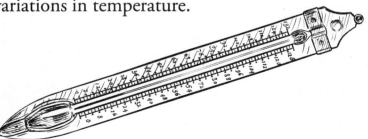

A 1714 thermometer

Aristotle (384–322 BC)

Aristotle was a philosopher who lived in ancient Greece. Throughout his life, he wrote about many topics including science, economics, politics, biology, and psychology.

In addition to laying the foundation for meteorology, Aristotle advanced science in many ways, including his early concepts of physics, his system for classifying living organisms, and his ideas on zoology (the study of animal behavior).

Aristotle even started a school in Athens, Greece, where he not only taught about science but helped his students to achieve happiness in their lives.

The thermometer was created in 1709 by Daniel Gabriel Fahrenheit. A Dutch scientist and inventor, Fahrenheit created a scale to measure fixed points of temperature. Two of those points included the temperature of the human body (98.6 degrees Fahrenheit) and the freezing point of water (32 degrees Fahrenheit).

Daniel Gabriel Fahrenheit

Fahrenheit, the unit of temperature measurement, was named after him.

Though Italian astronomer Galileo Galilei had created a water thermoscope in 1593, in 1714 Fahrenheit invented the version filled with mercury (a slippery, naturally occurring chemical element) that is widely used in the present day.

In addition to playing a role in the greater understanding of meteorology, Aristotle's book

Meteorologica contained some of the earliest writings about tornadoes.

Aristotle believed tornadoes started as spinning wind trapped inside of clouds, and as the wind escaped, it pulled the clouds along to form a funnel shape. Aristotle's theory wasn't quite right, but he didn't have any of the tools to fully understand tornadoes at the time. And we are still learning about tornadoes, and how they form, today.

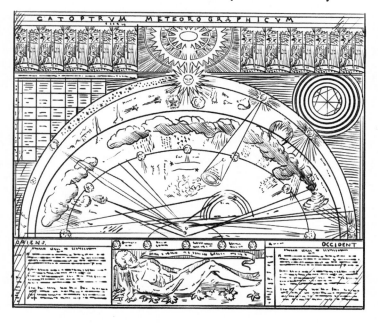

A 1623 meteorological chart based on Aristotle's *Meteorologica*

CHAPTER 2
How Tornadoes Form

Tornadoes are sneaky. They can form quickly and without warning. In fact, when a tornado first forms, it's invisible. At their core, tornadoes are powerful spinning columns of wind and air. It's only after they pick up dirt or other objects that we can see tornadoes with the naked eye.

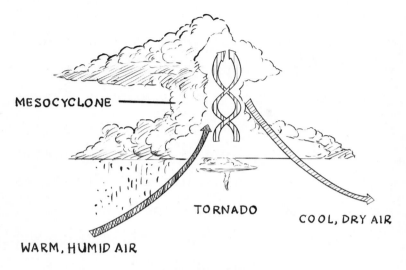

MESOCYCLONE ─────

TORNADO

COOL, DRY AIR

WARM, HUMID AIR

Anatomy of a supercell

The most common type of tornado begins as part of a supercell thunderstorm, a weather system with rotating winds. Supercells form when an updraft of warm and moist air shoots upward into the atmosphere. This sudden updraft creates a rotating area within the thunderstorm strong enough to trigger a tornado warning. The rotating mass of air is called a mesocyclone, and it's the very beginning of most tornadoes.

A tornado forms when moist, warm winds collide with dry, cold winds. As these weather patterns come together, the warm air rises over the cold air and cools as it goes up into the sky. As the air falls back down, it begins to spin. Imagine a clothes dryer as it tumbles the laundry end over end. That's exactly how a tornado begins. As the winds spin faster, a funnel shape forms in the air. When one end of the wind funnel touches the rotating mesocyclone, and the other end touches the ground, it's officially declared a tornado.

Tornadoes may last only minutes, like the one that struck Tinker Air Force Base in 1948. But some last for hours. A twister's strength and duration depend on the weather conditions inside and around the supercell thunderstorm that created it. Powerful supercells are not limited in the number of tornadoes they can produce. Some supercells are large weather systems that spawn multiple tornadoes over the course of minutes or hours.

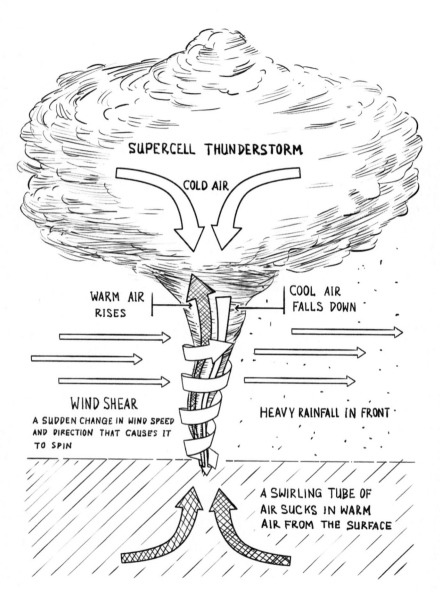

Anatomy of a tornado

When multiple tornadoes form from a single supercell, it's known as a "tornado outbreak." Such outbreaks are responsible for the worst tornado-related destruction in history.

Tornadoes have touched down on every continent in the world except Antarctica. While tornadoes can form anywhere, they're most common in the United States. On average, more than one thousand tornadoes touch down in the United States each year during tornado season.

Tornado Alley isn't the only place a dangerous tornado can occur within the United States. There are three other geographical regions, also called "alleys," that scientists and meteorologists keep a close eye on.

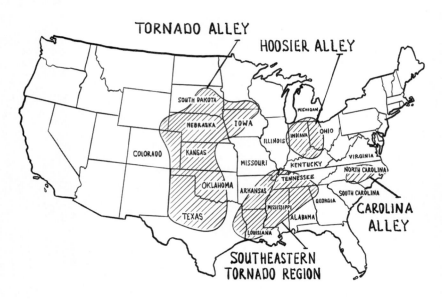

Carolina Alley

The least dangerous of all the alleys is Carolina Alley, which can be found in North and South Carolina. Carolina Alley produces an average of twenty to thirty tornadoes each year.

Hoosier Alley includes parts of Kentucky, Illinois, Indiana, Ohio, and Michigan. This area is slightly more dangerous than Carolina Alley, experiencing one to two hundred tornadoes each year.

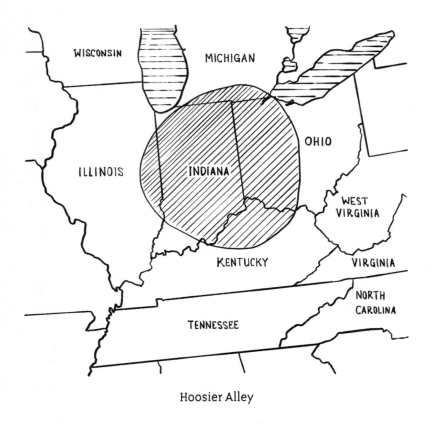

Hoosier Alley

While Tornado Alley may have the scariest of names, it's a stretch of land in the southeastern United States that earns the title of "most dangerous." Covering eastern Texas, Louisiana, Arkansas, Mississippi, Missouri, Tennessee, Alabama, and Georgia, this southeastern strip averages hundreds of tornadoes every year. Tornado Alley is responsible for producing 30 percent of all significant twisters in the United States, the southeastern region produces the most destructive ones. Why is that? The southern states are close to the humid weather of the Gulf Coast (the part of the Gulf of Mexico that forms a coastline along four of these states) and the constant dry winds that blow in from the west.

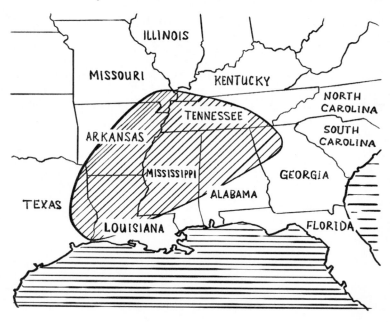

Southeastern Tornado Region

These weather fronts—air masses of different temperature and density—smash together over the southeastern region, allowing tornadoes to form at any time of year.

Many areas of the United States cool off at night, but the persistent warmth and humidity of the southern states means that many tornadoes in the region strike at night when residents are asleep and unable to react.

It's no secret that tornadoes can form anywhere; it's *why* they form that continues to baffle meteorologists. It's the same question that Fawbush and Miller wanted to answer in 1948.

CHAPTER 3
Predicting the Unpredictable

How tornadoes form is still a mystery to meteorologists. Scientists may understand the "recipe" for a tornado (what is needed to make them form), but it's impossible to predict which storms will produce them. The best tool for predicting these scary weather events is radar.

Radar, which stands for "radio detection and ranging," was created in the 1930s. A radar antenna sends out pulses of radio waves and receives back an "echo." This echo reveals whether a target is moving toward or away from the radar antenna. The technology was adopted by the military in 1940 to help track the movements of airplanes in the sky.

Radar detecting the movement of a plane

As with most early technologies, radar was not without its hiccups. Primitive radar systems didn't seem to function correctly in bad weather. Rather than show the locations of planes, the radar returned blurry images of large blobs. After a bit of confusion, scientists realized that the large masses only appeared on the display when it was raining nearby. What looked like blobs turned out to be wind and rain. The radar could detect or "see" weather that was invisible to humans! This discovery had few uses for the military but plenty in the world of weather prediction.

In 1942, the US Navy gifted the Weather

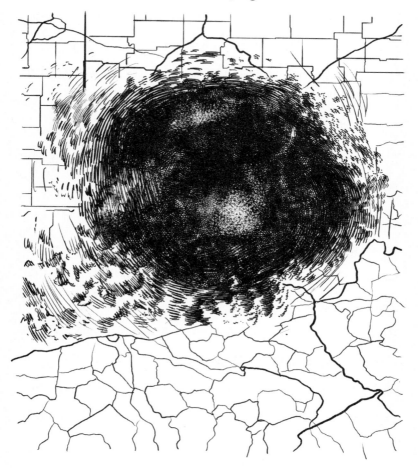

Bureau twenty-five radar antennas to help monitor weather across the United States. These early radar systems, along with maps and other data, were what Ernest Fawbush and Robert Miller had to work with at Tinker Air Force Base. These tools helped them make a very important decision on March 25, 1948, only five days after they had been caught off guard by the destructive tornado. As a supercell thunderstorm darkened the Oklahoma skies, the men finally convinced Commanding General Borum to issue a tornado forecast for the base.

This was a historic event. Before that day, weathermen could only warn of the potential for severe weather. The Weather Bureau policy banned the use of the word "tornado" in its forecasts. They wanted to keep people from panicking during bad storms.

The first-ever official tornado forecast was issued by Fawbush and Miller at three o'clock that afternoon. At the mention of the word *tornado*, soldiers at Tinker Air Force Base leaped into action. Men moved aircraft into hangars and tied down anything that could become a projectile in strong winds. After securing the base, soldiers were moved to safe locations.

Just as Fawbush and Miller predicted, another tornado roared through Tinker Air Force Base just three hours later. The storm hit hard, causing another $6 million in damage. Without Fawbush and Miller's warning, however, the outcome would have been much, much worse.

Major Ernest Fawbush and Captain Robert Miller
looking through weather reports

Following their momentous forecast, Fawbush
and Miller became celebrities in the weather-
prediction community. The pair found themselves
in charge of tornado prediction for most of
the central United States. Within three years,
Fawbush and Miller were leading the Air Force
Severe Weather Warning Center.

The National Weather Service

While it's known today as the National Weather Service, the agency was first named the Division of Telegrams and Reports for the Benefit of Commerce.

The National Weather Service logo

The weather service was founded by President Ulysses S. Grant on February 9, 1870. The decision was spurred by several weather-related disasters the same year, which sank hundreds of boats on the Great Lakes. President Grant felt it was important to observe weather at military stations and to monitor coastal regions to warn of approaching storms. Each day, "observing-sergeants" at twenty-two military installations across the United States reported on local weather.

In 1890, Congress renamed the agency the Weather Bureau. In 1970, the agency was given its final name: the National Weather Service.

Fawbush and Miller's work inspired the Weather Bureau to form the Severe Weather Unit in 1952. By 1953, it had been renamed the Severe Local Storms Warning Service (SELS). In 1995, SELS was renamed the Storm Prediction Center and became part of the National Severe Storms Laboratory (NSSL) in Norman, Oklahoma.

While it may seem strange that these weather-related agencies were renamed so often, the government's goal has always been to take advantage of the best technologies available and ensure the safety of the public.

Fawbush and Miller first used the phrase "Tornado Alley" in 1952 while conducting a research study of extreme weather in Texas, Colorado, and Nebraska. The men chose this name because the place where tornado activity was the highest was a lowland area settled between the Rocky Mountains and the Appalachian Mountains, thus creating a geographic "alley."

Between the mountains are the Great Plains, an expansive area of more than 1,125,000 square miles (roughly one-third of the United States) that are mostly flat and covered in prairies.

The name Tornado Alley became widely adopted five years later when it appeared in the headline of a *New York Times* article about tornadoes in the United States.

Radar technology slowly improved as Fawbush and Miller continued their work. The most common and reliable piece of technology used in weather prediction was Doppler radar. Named after Austrian mathematician and physicist Christian Doppler, the radar system revealed information on not only the position of the targets but also their movement. The early Doppler radar even provided the speed of targets, helping scientists predict a storm's specific time of arrival.

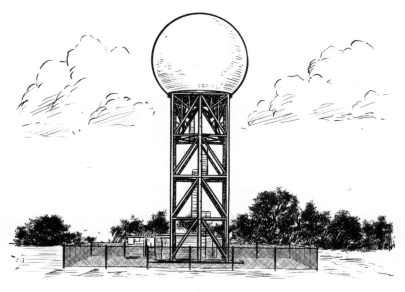

Modern Doppler radar dome

Christian Doppler (1803–1853)

Christian Andreas Doppler was born in Austria. Originally from a family of stone masons, Doppler discovered early in life that he didn't like stone nearly as much as he loved math. Rather than pursue the family trade, he became a mathematician and physicist. In 1842, Doppler first proposed what came to be known as the "Doppler effect."

In 1845, meteorologist and physicist Christophorus Buys Ballot held a demonstration in Holland, positioning a group of musicians next to a railroad track. As a train approached from a distance, the locomotive's whistle sounded high-pitched to the musicians. While the train passed by, its whistle sounded much lower in pitch. The musicians, who were trained to identify the difference in music notes, verified Doppler's theory.

Doppler's concept was applied to radar systems during World War II. By reading the "pitch" of a distant object, the radar could calculate how far a target was from the observers.

Radar wasn't the only practical application for Doppler's discovery. His technology is also found inside the radar guns that police officers use to determine a vehicle's speed. Remarkably, Doppler—a man born in the early 1800s—is helping to catch speeding drivers today.

But even the best radar systems and meteorologists sometimes make mistakes. Radar can't see a tornado. It can only see strong rotations in clouds, or debris that's flying around in a circular pattern. Even if meteorologists believe

a tornado may strike, they count on "ground truth" to verify the claims. Ground truth means that someone on the ground has seen the tornado with their own eyes.

The National Weather Service can't be everywhere at once to see tornadoes when they touch down. The organization has relied on storm spotters to provide ground truth since the 1970s as part of a volunteer program called SKYWARN.

Storm spotters are citizens who are trained to watch for storms, particularly in rural areas. When a storm spotter sees weather patterns that could potentially be dangerous, they take photographs and videos.

SKYWARN

SKYWARN was founded in the early 1970s by the National Weather Service to promote public safety. The organization trains citizens how to watch for, and report, severe-storm data. When a severe-weather watch is reported, members of SKYWARN head outside to make observations and record their data.

Anyone can become a SKYWARN storm spotter by taking a two-hour class presented by a certified representative of the National Weather Service. To date, there are as many as 400,000 trained storm spotters across the United States.

By sharing the footage with local meteorologists, storm spotters help provide advance warning of severe storms and tornadoes in order to save lives.

Of course, tornadoes aren't the only life-threatening type of storm we regularly experience in the United States.

CHAPTER 4
Tornadoes and Other Weather Threats

While tornadoes are dangerous and terrifying events, they aren't the only way that air and wind can come together to create a destructive force.

Believe it or not, tornadoes can also form over water. Waterspouts form when cold air moves across warm bodies of water. Much like with the formation of a tornado, the winds meet, begin to spin, and then form a vortex. Despite most waterspouts lasting mere minutes, they can create their own types of danger and damage.

Some waterspouts form over water but then jump onto land. Tornadic waterspouts, as they are known, damage boats, homes, and docks along the shore. These waterspouts are often accompanied by high winds, hail, and lightning. When they do move onto land, a tornado warning is issued for the area.

A waterspout

Fair weather waterspouts are weaker and form farther out in the ocean and away from land. Without high winds to carry them along, they often stay in one location. If a fair weather waterspout does move onto shore, it quickly dissolves. More waterspouts form off the coast of Florida than anywhere else in the world.

Another wind-based event happens most

often in desert regions. Dust devils form when cool air meets heat from surfaces such as concrete, creating pockets of swirling air. Like a tornado, a dust devil spins quickly, collecting dirt and debris until it runs out of warm air and vanishes.

A dust devil

Dust devils can grow from ten feet to three hundred feet across and up to one thousand feet high. While they lack the destructive power of a tornado, dust devils can damage structures, vehicles, and power lines.

When cold winds blow across warm, tropical waters in the ocean, a different type of weather event happens. The low-pressure system created by the wind feeds on warm air, creating a closed-circulation air mass that spins faster and faster. This process forms what is known as a "cell." If the winds are less than thirty-nine miles per hour, the cell is called a tropical depression. Once winds reach a speed of thirty-nine miles per hour, the weather cell becomes a tropical storm and is given a name by the World Meteorological Organization. If the weather cell's wind speeds reach seventy-four miles per hour, it's classified as one of the planet's most fearsome storms: a hurricane.

A hurricane as seen from above

The most dangerous hurricanes are made of winds whipping around at over 180 miles per hour. A powerful hurricane can last for days, causing flooding and catastrophic damage to homes and communities. Once over land, hurricanes run out of warm air, weakening before they finally dissolve.

One of a hurricane's defining characteristics is its eye, a small area of clear weather in its center. However, this eye is surrounded by the eyewall, where a hurricane's winds are the strongest.

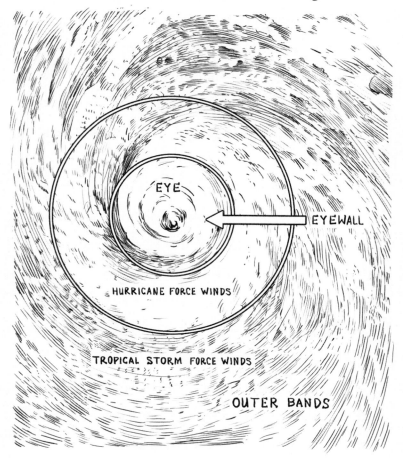

The anatomy of a hurricane

What's the Difference Between a Tornado and a Hurricane?

Tornadoes and hurricanes are both masses of rotating wind, but there are key differences between them. For instance, hurricanes form over warm tropical waters, while tornadoes form over land. Hurricanes are larger, less frequent, and slower than tornadoes.

Hurricanes can be up to three hundred miles wide, while an average tornado is only three to five hundred yards in width. An average of seven to ten hurricanes form from tropical storms each year in the Atlantic Ocean, while as many as eight hundred to one thousand tornadoes appear in the United States in the same time frame.

Hurricanes can last days or weeks, while most tornadoes spend less than one hour on the ground. Hurricane winds are often less than 180 miles per hour. A tornado's winds can reach speeds of three hundred miles per hour or more! Hurricanes form slowly, providing days of warning for those in their path, but tornadoes form quickly, and those in danger may only have several minutes to react.

Most tornadoes form in the spring and summer months, with the peak season lasting from March through July. Hurricanes become a threat in the summer and fall months, with the official season lasting from June through November.

Hurricane

Tornado

In the Southern Hemisphere, hurricanes spin clockwise. In the Northern Hemisphere, they spin counterclockwise. These storms also carry different labels depending on where they formed. Hurricanes are storms that have formed in the North Atlantic or central and eastern North Pacific. Similar storms that form in the western North Pacific are called typhoons. Those that form in the South Pacific and Indian Ocean are called cyclones.

Hurricane-force winds don't only come from hurricanes. *Derechos*, named for the Spanish word meaning "straight," are a straight-line windstorm. Derechos move quickly, battering communities with strong winds, heavy rains, and flooding. A storm is classified as a derecho when wind damage covers a total distance of more than 240 miles with wind gusts of fifty-eight miles per hour or greater.

A derecho

The Earth's Hemispheres

The Earth is separated into four hemispheres: north, south, east, and west.

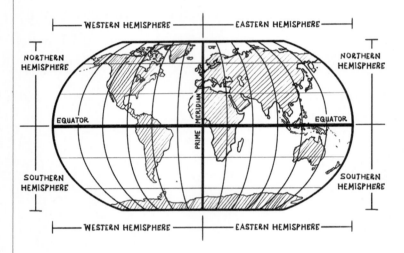

The equator, an imaginary line that stretches horizontally across the center, divides the planet into the Northern and Southern Hemispheres. The Northern Hemisphere is home to the continents of North America, Europe, northern South America, northern Africa, and most of Asia. Continents including South America, Australia, Antarctica, parts of Africa, and some Asian islands such as Indonesia are found in the Southern Hemisphere.

The imaginary line dividing Earth into the Eastern and Western Hemispheres runs from the North Pole to the South Pole and is called the Prime Meridian. The North and South Americas, Antarctica, and parts of Europe and Africa are in the Western Hemisphere, while Asia, Australia, and other parts of Europe and Africa are found in the Eastern Hemisphere.

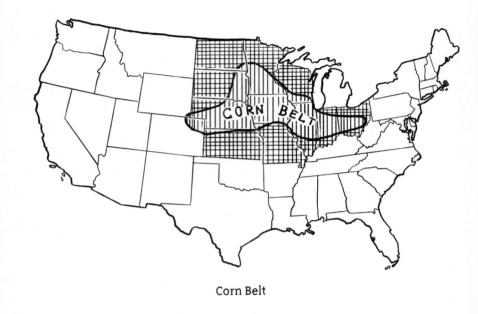

Corn Belt

Derechos occur in the spring and summer months. These windstorms most commonly form in the "Corn Belt," which stretches from the upper Mississippi Valley southeast into the Ohio Valley. Like most storms, derechos are formed by the collision of warm air and moist air. While tornadoes, waterspouts, and dust devils may only swirl around for minutes, derechos can last for days.

While these storms each have their own folklore surrounding them, tornadoes might just hold the record for the highest number of associated myths.

For instance, there are people who believe that tornadoes will never strike the same place twice. This is not true. The town of Codell, Kansas, was struck by a tornado on the same day, May 20, for three consecutive years, from 1916 through 1918!

Another common myth is that tornadoes won't cross hills or mountains. Many residents in Topeka, Kansas, believed that one-thousand-

Sculpture memorial to the May 20 tornadoes

foot-high Burnett's Mound would protect them

from twisters. But on June 8, 1966, a tornado crossed the mound, killing seventeen people and causing more than $200 million in damage.

Tornado hits Topeka, Kansas, 1966

Another myth is that during a tornado, you should hide in the southwest corner of your basement. Why? Due to the jet stream—strong gusts of wind that blow west to east high above the United States—most storms move in a northeastern direction. This myth assumes that if a tornado strikes a home, the structure will collapse to the northeast—and away from those who are hiding. Experts disagree. And weather doesn't always follow the rules. Buildings do not collapse in any specific direction during a tornado.

Regardless of what studies have taught us about various dangerous weather patterns, storms remain incredibly unpredictable. Some tornadoes are small and cause little to no damage. Others can cause destruction on an unimaginable scale.

CHAPTER 5
Nature's Fury

As tornadoes grabbed the curiosity of scientists in the United States—and technology made sharing data between locations easier—additional organizations were established to track and study weather. This culminated in the founding of NOAA, the National Oceanic and Atmospheric Administration, in 1970.

NOAA, which still exists today, is responsible for monitoring atmospheric and oceanic conditions, charting seas, exploring the ocean depths, regulating fishing, managing the protection of marine animals, and forecasting the weather.

After spending decades recording tornado data, scientists sought new ways to study and classify them. In 1971, meteorologist Tetsuya Theodore Fujita presented his Fujita Scale, also known as the F-Scale, which classified tornadoes based on their wind speeds.

Fujita's scale ranked tornadoes on a scale of zero to five based on both wind speed and the amount of damage left behind by a twister.

FUJITA SCALE		
F-0	40 - 72 MPH WINDS	MINOR
F-1	73 - 112 MPH	MODERATE
F-2	113 - 157 MPH	STRONG
F-3	158 - 206 MPH	SEVERE
F-4	207 - 260 MPH	DEVASTATING
F-5	261 - 318 MPH	INCREDIBLE

According to Fujita's chart, an F-0 tornado clocked wind speeds of less than 73 miles per hour and caused little damage. An F-5 tornado, however, carried winds of 261 miles per hour or greater. An F-5 tornado could easily destroy an entire city in minutes.

Fujita's F-Scale helped meteorologists learn

much about tornadoes, but scientists wanted even more specific data. In 2007, NOAA adopted the Enhanced Fujita Scale, which provided more precise rules to classify tornadoes and the damage they leave behind. On this new "EF-Scale," an EF-0 tornado has wind speeds of up to eighty-five miles per hour but causes limited amounts of damage. An EF-5 tornado causes catastrophic damage with winds slicing through trees and structures at more than two hundred miles per hour.

ENHANCED FUJITA SCALE		
EF-0	65 - 85 MPH WINDS	MINOR
EF-1	86 - 110 MPH	MODERATE
EF-2	111 - 135 MPH	STRONG
EF-3	136 - 165 MPH	SEVERE
EF-4	166 - 200 MPH	DEVASTATING
EF-5	>200 MPH	INCREDIBLE

Tetsuya Fujita (1920–1998)

Tetsuya "Ted" Fujita, also known as "Mr. Tornado" by his friends, was a Japanese American meteorologist and inventor of the Fujita Scale.

Fujita lived in the city of Kokura, Japan, during World War II. After the war, Fujita studied the damage of the atomic bombs dropped over Hiroshima and Nagasaki. He realized that the damage caused by the bombs, and that of tornadoes, was very similar. Becoming highly interested in severe weather, Fujita moved to the United States in 1953 specifically to study tornadoes.

Fujita spent his career researching and teaching at the University of Chicago. As part of his studies, he visited the aftermath of countless tornadoes. He surveyed the destruction from on high in airplanes and walked the damage paths on the ground. He discovered that the direction in which trees had fallen in a storm could help scientists track the path of a twister. Fujita also pored over thousands of photos of tornadoes frame by frame, teaching himself how to read wind speeds. His research resulted in his creation of the Fujita Scale, adopted in 1971.

The first EF-5 tornado ever recorded on the new Enhanced Fujita Scale occurred in Greensburg, Kansas, in 2007. The storm injured more than sixty people, left eleven dead, and destroyed more than 95 percent of the city.

As scientists reclassified past tornadoes using the Enhanced Fujita Scale, many of the worst storms in history fell into the new EF-5 category.

The Tri-State Tornado, recorded in March 1925, touched down twenty-three years before the work of Fawbush and Miller. The twister lasted three and a half hours. During that time, the tornado traveled 219 miles across Missouri, Illinois, and Indiana, killing almost seven hundred people.

The Glazier-Higgins-Woodward tornado outbreak of April 1947 is another example of one supercell producing multiple tornadoes. The worst of these was an EF-5 that traveled more than 125 miles through Texas and Oklahoma. The tornado outbreak killed nearly two hundred people, and it could have been much worse. An electric worker in Woodward, Oklahoma, named Erwin Walker braved the storm to cut the city's power lines just moments before the tornado struck. Despite being killed in the storm, Walker's quick thinking kept live power lines from being tossed about by the tornado, which undoubtedly saved many lives.

Damage caused by Glazier-Higgins-Woodward Tornado

The Super Outbreak of 2011 brought with it more than 340 tornadoes that touched down in twenty-one different states over four scary days. These tornadoes caused more than $12 billion in damage and left 321 dead. It was Alabama that took the brunt of the outbreak. On April 27, the state was struck by sixty-two tornadoes in just twenty-four hours! During the storm, there were as many as six tornadoes on the ground at a given time. Four of these tornadoes were classified as EF-5s. In all of Alabama's prior history, EF-5 tornadoes were recorded no more than once a year.

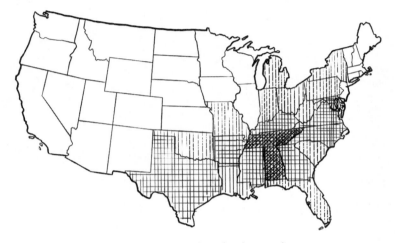

The 2011 Super Outbreak of tornadoes

Just a month later in May 2011, an EF-5 tornado struck Joplin, Missouri. At its strongest, the tornado was more than one mile wide. During its thirty-eight minutes on the ground, the twister killed 161 people, injured more than 1,100, and caused more than $2.8 billion in damage.

The Joplin Tornado battered more than eight thousand buildings, destroying more than half of those it touched. It remains the single costliest tornado in US history.

On May 31, 2013, an EF-5 tornado struck the city of El Reno, Oklahoma. At 2.6 miles across, it holds the record for the widest tornado ever recorded. At the peak of the storm, the tornado's winds clocked in at over three hundred miles per hour. The El Reno Tornado caused injuries to 151 people. The vortex (its swirling movement) zigged and zagged during its time on the ground. This behavior made the storm's path impossible to predict and caused the deaths of eight people.

El Reno Tornado, 2013

Planning for a tornado can make a difficult experience easier for everyone. Tornadoes can cause massive damage to both life and property. And while it may seem obvious that it's better to hide from a tornado than to go out and chase it, there are people who do exactly that.

What to Do When a Tornado Strikes

The current average tornado warning time in the United States is thirteen minutes. Although tornadoes can be very frightening, being prepared and having a plan in place when each second counts can help anyone better survive a storm.

People living in Tornado Alley know that twisters can appear at any time. As storms darken the skies, TV weather forecasters may announce a tornado watch. (A tornado watch is issued when conditions are right to produce a tornado. But it does not mean a tornado has formed.)

If a town or city has them, tornado sires will sound when storm winds reach seventy miles per hour, or if a radar reveals an immediate threat. The loud, wailing sirens indicate that people should go indoors immediately.

A tornado watch becomes a tornado warning

when a twister is developing in the skies. The safest place to be during a tornado is inside a storm cellar—a large, metal room buried in the ground. These cellars are designed to hold essential survival items and to keep people safe.

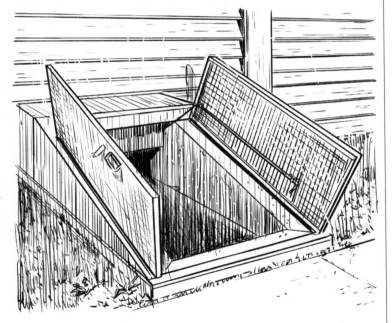

If a storm cellar isn't available, the next safest place is in a basement, beneath a stairwell, or in a room without windows, like a closet or bathroom.

CHAPTER 6
Chasing the Storm

Tornado Alley is a hotspot for storm chasers: scientists, meteorologists, and ordinary citizens who intentionally drive toward storms and tornadoes instead of away from them.

The reasons for putting their lives at risk are

different for each chaser. Some want to learn more about how tornadoes work in hopes of using that knowledge to save lives. Some like the thrill. Others capture close-up photos and videos of tornadoes to sell them to news stations.

The most professional storm chasers drive heavy-duty trucks covered in armor. Inside, the vehicles are filled with scientific instruments such as radar, radios, and GPS equipment. The life of a storm chaser is not for the faint of heart.

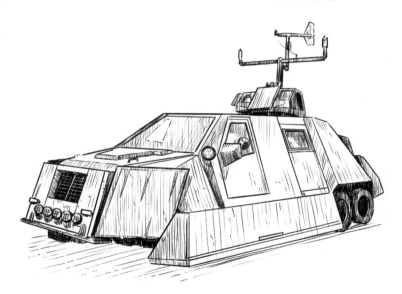

Custom-built storm-chaser vehicle

Benjamin Franklin

Storm chasing isn't a new idea. People have chased tornadoes since as far back as 1755. Benjamin Franklin, the scientist, inventor, writer, and statesman who went on to become an architect of the Declaration of Independence in 1776, was an early storm chaser.

While out riding a horse one spring afternoon in the Maryland countryside, Franklin saw a "whirlwind" cross the road ahead of him. The funnel grew bigger before his eyes and took off over a hill. Filled with curiosity, Franklin chased it on horseback.

Benjamin Franklin had a reputation for allowing his curiosity to get the better of him, especially in dangerous situations. Three years earlier, Franklin completed his famous experiment in which he flew a kite in a thunderstorm. Attached to the kite was a metal key. He tried to prove that the key would attract lightning. The experiment set the stage for his invention of the lightning rod.

As Franklin chased the tornado, he pulled a whip from his saddlebag. He cracked the whip at the funnel, hoping to "break" it. Instead, the twister veered into the woods, where it kicked up leaves and snapped tree branches.

Franklin retreated from the danger, wowed by the whirlwind's power.

The most successful storm chaser in history

is probably David Hoadley, who was born in 1938 in Spencer, Indiana. As a child, Hoadley developed an interest in storms. He preferred watching bad weather through the window over more common children's activities. Hoadley was just ten years old when Fawbush and Miller were having their scientific breakthroughs in tornado research. It was after a twister plowed through Bismarck, North Dakota, where Hoadley's family had moved, that the "father of storm chasing" found his obsession. Upon graduating high school, Hoadley joined the military. In 1963, he asked to be stationed at Fort Riley in Kansas. Hoadley knew this would put him exactly where he wanted to be—in the middle of Tornado Alley.

David Hoadley

Any time a major storm kicked up, Hoadley grabbed his camera and snapped as many photos as possible. When video cameras became easily accessible in the 1980s, Hoadley recorded every tornado he could. His photographs have been published in countless magazines, and his videos have been studied by scientists all over the world.

Due to Hoadley's persistence when it came to recording tornadoes, his contributions have greatly advanced the study of these weather events.

In the earliest days, Hoadley was known as a "cloud watcher." As the hobby became more popular, the term "storm chaser" came into use, which sounded more adventurous. Hoadley founded the newsletter *Stormtrack* in 1977 as more and more storm chasers appeared in Tornado Alley. The publication, which still exists today, served as a platform to share tornado information with amateur and professional chasers alike. Throughout his career, Hoadley has witnessed more than two hundred tornadoes and has driven more than 750,000 miles chasing them.

While many storm chasers watch tornadoes from the ground, others have studied them from the air.

Physicist Stirling Colgate had always been interested in destruction. Thunderstorms.

Stirling Colgate

Explosions. Nuclear power. In the 1940s, Colgate worked for the federal government on top secret projects like the atomic bomb. After retiring in the 1980s, Colgate spent his final years pursuing his biggest interest: tornadoes.

Hoping to learn what happens inside of a twister—and maybe even how to destroy them—Colgate built small rockets filled with scientific instruments. His plan was to fire the rockets from a plane into tornadoes. Airplane pilots thought Colgate's idea was not practical and too dangerous. Colgate knew how to fly, so he decided to do it himself.

Colgate trained for his experiment in the Florida Keys. He chased waterspouts in his Cessna

210 airplane and practiced firing his rockets. After several weeks of run-throughs, he felt he was ready to tackle tornadoes.

Taking to the skies of Tornado Alley, Colgate spent the next few years chasing twisters. Despite his best efforts, the rockets that he fired from his Cessna never hit their targets. The heavy winds from the tornadoes whipped the small rockets away as if they were toys. Rather than give up, Colgate tried harder.

While chasing a tornado over Pampa, Texas, in 1982, the scientist was determined to make sure his rockets reached the funnel. After missing the first several shots, Colgate flew closer to the tornado. Suddenly, Colgate found himself dangerously close to the twister. The tornado changed direction, roaring directly at Colgate's plane. As the scientist was about to fire his final rocket, a sudden downdraft pushed his plane violently toward the ground.

Colgate regained control of the airplane just seconds away from crashing. He made an emergency landing in a field and vowed to never fly close to tornadoes again.

Every tornado season, thousands of storm

chasers converge on Tornado Alley. They all hope to see the biggest tornado. To get the best photo. To learn something new. To feel the sense of adventure that keeps them coming back, season after season. Tourists can even book tornado adventures where they ride with fearless storm chasers and maybe see a tornado firsthand.

The interest in storm chasing has only grown in recent decades. Films like *Twister* made storm chasing look adventuresome. Reality TV shows like the Discovery Channel's *Storm Chasers* and the independent series *Tornado Chasers* spotlight both the peril and the excitement.

Twister

Capitalizing on the storm-chasing sensation, the blockbuster action movie *Twister* was released in 1996. In the film, storm chasers Doctor Jo Harding and Bill Harding (played by actors Helen Hunt and Bill Paxton) try to release sensors into a live tornado to learn more about how they work. The goal of the scientists is to increase warning times—and safety—for the public. When a tornado outbreak strikes Oklahoma, the chasers see their big opportunity.

Twister earned more than $40 million in its opening weekend, becoming the second highest-grossing movie of 1996. At the time, the movie pushed the limits of computer-generated imagery to bring its massive, frightening tornadoes to the big screen. *Twister* also holds the distinction of being the first film to be released on DVD in the United States.

The new film, *Twisters*, was released in 2024.

Tim Samaras

As thrilling as chasing a tornado sounds, it's a dangerous activity.

Engineer Tim Samaras was a noted storm chaser and star of the *Storm Chasers* reality show. Samaras became involved with storms because he wanted to learn about the inner workings of tornadoes. He even designed and built his own weather instruments and probes (called "turtles") and shared his data with the scientific community.

Samaras's research served as an inspiration for the characters and story in the film *Twister*.

In 2013, Samaras, his son Paul, and meteorologist Carl Young chased the El Reno Tornado in Oklahoma. Samaras's goal was to deploy his homemade probes to learn more about the

EF-5 twister that raged across the landscape. When the tornado changed direction, Samaras and the others were unable to escape. It was the first time in known history that chasers had been killed by a tornado.

In recent years, weather patterns around the world have become more unpredictable. Tornado Alley is no exception. The future of storm chasing is more unknown—and more dangerous—than ever before.

CHAPTER 7
The Future of the Storm

It's no secret that the climate on planet Earth is changing in many dramatic ways. Since the 1880s, average temperatures around the world have gone up nearly two degrees Fahrenheit.

A forest wildfire

Those two degrees are more significant than they sound: They trigger fewer colder days and more warmer ones. That means fewer record low temperatures and more record highs. Glaciers around the world are melting at a faster pace, causing sea levels to rise. There is an increase in wildfires and also in the number of droughts.

Above all, this change in climate means more warm air floating around the jet stream that can be converted into the beginnings of dangerous hurricanes and tornadoes. This influx of warmer air from climate change means that tornado season will start earlier and last longer. Tornado seasons over the past decade have been stronger, more deadly, and more unpredictable than ever.

A 2018 study conducted by NOAA discovered that tornadoes are declining in numbers within Tornado Alley and increasing in eastern states. Is Tornado Alley on the move? Places that rarely saw tornadoes are now being ravaged by twisters.

Within a few years, Tornado Alley may change its location on the map entirely, as states including Arkansas, Mississippi, Tennessee, Kentucky, Georgia, and Alabama experience more tornado outbreaks than ever before.

Tornadoes reported in 2018

This is bad news for humans. The eastern states that are being pummeled by more and more twisters contain large rural areas, but the population of those areas has dramatically increased in recent years. Where once a tornado may have hit a forest or farmland, more people will now be in the path of danger.

But as our planet's climate continues to warm and change, will any place really be safe? Even if families choose to live where tornadoes aren't a common problem, hurricanes, dust devils, and derechos seem to all be appearing more frequently.

Luckily, the US government is working hard to counteract climate change. By instituting laws and regulations, the United States Environmental Protection Agency (EPA) hopes to help significantly slow or reverse the warming trends of the planet.

It's believed that the biggest causes of climate change come from the manufacturing industries and the vehicles we drive.

Factories, power plants, and even cars and trucks give off harmful gases that pollute the air, contaminate water, destroy crops, and damage the ozone layer (the invisible shield in the Earth's stratosphere that protects our planet from the sun's rays). These gases are harmful to humans and animals and are believed to damage the lungs, heart, skin, kidneys, and they can sometimes cause cancer.

Government agencies such as the EPA have worked to pass laws that will limit pollution or force the development and use of cleaner alternatives. Unfortunately, the process is slow, and the results of these changes may not be seen for years or even decades.

The Environmental Protection Agency

Established in 1970 by President Richard Nixon, the United States Environmental Protection Agency is an independent agency within the US government. The EPA is responsible for conducting environmental assessment, research, and education.

The goal of the EPA is to protect the health of both humans and the environment. The agency does so by enforcing various environmental laws and issuing fines to people or companies that don't follow the rules.

Employees of the EPA include engineers, environmental protection specialists, and scientists.

To prevent and reverse climate change, everyone in the world must do their part. In the future, more people will drive half-gasoline, half-electric hybrid cars. More homeowners will install solar panels to power their homes. Factories will

switch to water-based hydropower, and more power plants will harness wind to generate energy. Steps like these can create a safer environment and a more stable planet.

While global warming affects the entire world, Tornado Alley covers just 15 percent of the continental United States. But it's within that area that 30 percent of all significant tornadoes occur. Because Tornado Alley is home to some very large cities—Dallas, Texas; Oklahoma City, Oklahoma; Omaha, Nebraska; and Kansas City,

Missouri; and Wichita, Kansas, among others—it means that more than seventeen million people are potentially in harm's way.

It might surprise you to learn that despite tornadoes being a constant threat, building codes (the specifications to which homes and businesses must be built) in Tornado Alley are not different than anywhere else in the United States.

Believe it or not, only one city in Tornado Alley—Moore, Oklahoma—has passed building-requirement regulations to strengthen homes against the frequent storms. As our planet's weather continues to worsen, we may see other cities follow Moore's lead.

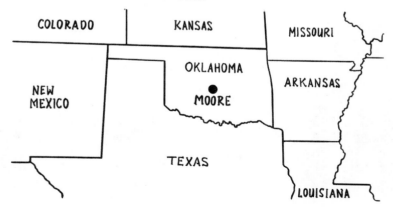

And even as we fight to lower the planet's rising temperatures, tornadoes will always be waiting to surprise us. The best thing that we can do is be prepared.

Timeline of Tornado Alley

1925 — The Tri-State Tornado leaves a two-hundred-mile trail of damage across Missouri, Illinois, and Indiana

1947 — A 1.8-mile-wide tornado rips through Woodward, Oklahoma, destroying the city

1948 — Major Ernest Fawbush and Captain Robert Miller deliver the first-ever tornado forecast

1952 — Fawbush and Miller first use the phrase "Tornado Alley"

1971 — Meteorologist Tetsuya "Ted" Fujita introduces the Fujita Scale to rate tornado intensity

1977 — *Stormtrack*, the newsletter for early storm chasers, is founded by David Hoadley

1996 — *Twister* is released in theaters and becomes the second highest–grossing film of the year

2007 — The Enhanced Fujita Scale is adopted by the US

2011 — A Super Outbreak sees over 340 tornadoes touch down in twenty-one states over the course of four days

2018 — A weather study suggests that the number of tornadoes in Tornado Alley is decreasing, while the number in the southeastern United States is rising

2024 — The new film, *Twisters*, is released in movie theaters

Timeline of the World

1925 — New York City becomes the most populated city in the world at the time

1939 — The official search for female aviator Amelia Earhart is called off after her disappearance two years earlier

1947 — Kenneth Arnold makes the first reported UFO sighting near Mount Rainier, Washington, beginning the modern era of UFO sightings

1952 — The United States Army division of Special Forces, which undertakes the most dangerous combat and rescue missions, is created

1964 — The Civil Rights Act is signed into law by US president Lyndon B. Johnson

1977 — The Atari 2600 is released in North America, changing home video-game consoles forever

2007 — Apple cofounder Steve Jobs reveals the very first iPhone model to the world

2013 — The Indian Space Research Organization successfully launches the *Mangalyaan* spacecraft to orbit Mars

2019 — Automobile manufacturer Bugatti announces the most expensive car ever made. It costs $19 million, and only one is produced

2023 — The US military shoots down an alleged Chinese spy balloon off the coast of South Carolina

Bibliography

*Books for young readers

*Crane, Cody. *All About Tornadoes: Discovering Earth's Strongest Winds*. New York: Scholastic, 2022.

Cross, Kim. *What Stands in a Storm: A True Story of Love and Resilience in the Worst Superstorm in History*. New York: Atria Publishing Group, 2016.

Davidson, Keay. *Twister: The Science of Tornadoes and the Making of an Adventure Movie*. New York: Pocket Books, 1996.

*Herman, Gail. *What Is Climate Change?* New York: Penguin Workshop, 2018.

*Meister, Cari. *Disaster Zone: Tornadoes*. Minneapolis, MN: Jump! Inc., 2016.

Price, Jay M., Sadonia Corns, Jessica Nellis, Craig Torbenson, and Keith Wondra. *Kansas: In the Heart of Tornado Alley. Images of America*. Charleston, SC: Arcadia Publishing, 2011.

*Rathburn, Betsy. *Tornadoes. Natural Disasters*. Minneapolis, MN: Bellweather Media, 2020.

Websites

National Oceanic and Atmospheric Administration. www.noaa.gov

National Weather Service. www.weather.gov

United States Environmental Protection Agency. www.epa.gov